Leadership Nuts

LEADERSHIP LESSONS FOUND IN NATURE

52 CONCISE ESSAYS

Leadership Nuts

LEADERSHIP LESSONS FOUND IN NATURE

FRESH LEADERSHIP
NUTS FOUND ONLY
IN NATURE

LMTD EDTN

NUTS LEADERSHIP

100% NATURAL INGRED. | 52 OZ.

SLIGHTLY OFF THE BEATEN PATH

LEIGH FARROW

NASHVILLE, TENNESSEE

Book Cover/Interior/eBook Design by The Book Cover Whisperer: ProfessionalBookCoverDesign.com

Book Cover Illustration by Jeffrey Crutchfield

Interior Illustrations by Charlie Wetherington

978-1-7353383-2-3 Paperback
978-1-7353383-0-9 Hardcover
978-1-7353383-1-6 eBook

Printed in the United States of America

FIRST EDITION

For Marc

There is…
The heady smell of earth and fish,
The tea colored water as it laps onto rocky shore,
The murmur of the pyramidal cedars in a light breeze,
And you.

Contents

Foreword

Do you have any idea what crows, an armadillo, a red/white fishing bobber, dandelions or black vultures can teach you about leadership? I didn't either until I read *Leadership Nuts*. If you want to discover what 52 protagonists in nature have to do with your leadership development, read on.

In my career, as an interim CEO or CIO with different companies across diverse industries, I quickly became a student of leadership. In order to effect the changes or goals as the interim "new guy," I needed to rely not only on my own leadership but upon that of others as well. I obviously did not have all the knowledge needed to lead and evolve the organization, so it was incumbent upon me to quickly identify those key contributors with the right leadership attributes and encourage and empower them to "get things done." I wish I would have had this book early in my career!

In her essays, Leigh sets forth the most concise and relevant list of leadership traits, issues, and even mistakes that I have encountered. She uses a broad spectrum of nature's residents and elements as metaphors to artfully illustrate varying leadership topics, each accompanied by concise advice and action items for success. In doing so, Leigh's words cement an image and a lesson in an indelible way. What a uniquely creative way to observe and learn.

I believe this book will speak to any individual who desires to build upon or enhance their leadership competence. It will serve as a resource for teams looking to improve performance, strengthen communication, and embrace accountability. The metaphors will raise awareness of issues and add perspective. Families could also benefit from these coachable lessons.

These insightful essays will enlighten you and elevate your awareness so that in the future you will find it difficult to observe nature's multitude of creatures and events without a leadership lesson coming to mind. I predict that you will read the book more than once.

~Bruce Rhoades

INTRODUCTION

Walking beneath the tree canopy of winding country roads, across rocky ridge-top trails, and along lake-edged trodden paths, I shed the layers of a successful career. Through the course of my cadence, I recalled the people I had the privilege, or pain, of working alongside, the decisions I had made or that were made for me, and the joys or grievances I still carried. As I walked from past into present, my sensibilities shifted. I began to see a correlation between Mother Nature and the leadership ideals to which I had aspired throughout my career. Her inhabitants survive on instinct and are industrious, clever, and entertaining; her flora is resilient, unique, and significant; and her elements dependable, passionate, and awe-inspiring. I saw the dark side of her ferocity, fear and foes as the challenges and pitfalls I encountered while working to become a better leader, a better person. These essays are a culmination of my observations and ponderings while wandering through Western Kentucky and Middle Tennessee.

Whatever your path in life, I invite you to experience the leadership lessons to be found when you dare to step outside.

Leadership Nuts

Indecision

The leaves of crimson and yellow floated on the cool, crisp air, signaling the change of season. With winter approaching, the red squirrel, not given to hibernation, was busy stockpiling food to survive the cold months ahead. Unfortunately, at times, this singular focus comes at a cost. Case in point, the squirrel, nut firmly in its mouth, darts into the road and dances the dance of indecision that abruptly concludes with dire consequences.

Does this personify your leadership style? Are you goal-driven, but fall victim to indecisiveness, second-guessing, or reversing direction at that critical moment? If so, consider the reason. Do you consider too many opinions, worry about the unknown, or are you just bogged down in analysis? Whatever the pretext, to not make the decision is the decision—and that comes at a cost to you, the team, and the organization. Turn things around, be vulnerable, and seek advice from someone you trust. Filter outside noise, believe in your instincts, or, if nothing else, flip a coin. Commit to being decisive; otherwise, that nut does you no good if you cannot make it across the street.

Thick skin

The armored like vehicle lumbered down the hill, displaced leaves, and created quite the noise. Alerted to danger, the nine-banded armadillo braked hard and quickly burrowed into the ground, leaving only its hardened, plated exterior exposed. The natural armor of this barrel-shaped mammal serves to protect its tender underbelly from predators.

As a leader, have you developed a thick skin to protect your heart? Opinions, feedback, and criticism, from both above and below the line, are part and parcel of the job. To survive, and to not become hardened in the process, you must learn to differentiate between the meaningful and the irrelevant. Use patience to provide people the space to say what they need to say, discern what of the commentary is worthwhile, and move forward. Employ internal laughter to negate harsh, unhelpful narratives. Be keenly aware of the majority viewpoint and do not internalize the hyperbole of the minority. Your positive emotions are critical to the well-being of both you and your team, and you must learn to protect the vulnerable, empathetic, and kind aspects of your leadership. Develop an armor of thick skin, so when in the path of verbal challenge, you will easily survive the moment.

Happiness

Nature awoke in a monochromatic mood, liberally painting the day in tones of gray. The lack of color made walking in the woods feel mandatory rather than uplifting and the idea to quit gained ground. Quite suddenly a flash of brilliant blue pierced the sky as an eastern bluebird sailed past. The impact was immediate, as that tiny harbinger of happiness brought joy to the day. Bluebirds are a symbol of happiness, hope, and a better tomorrow.

As a leader, do you feel those things in equal measure to the bluebird? Often unrecognized as a leadership attribute, happiness is typically considered the goal rather than the starting point. A happy leader defines their responsibilities as a calling or a choice, rather than a sacrifice or a burden. Their positive behavior is contagious, triggers kindness, and influences the health of the organization. They build relationally strong teams that feel inclusive, recognized, and empowered—and have a voice. To begin the process, rediscover the joy in your work, lift up your team, and accomplish something, anything, that brings about success. Recognize that happiness is an internal superpower that does not require a cape, just a tiny pair of bluebird wings.

Building

The failing light of day afforded a moment's glimpse of the American beaver as it broke the water's surface. Gliding swiftly through the current, this large rodent is nature's true engineer. The beaver has the unique ability to forever alter the environment; often at odds with mankind, beavers create ponds, wetlands, and new ecosystems.

As a leader, what is your capacity to build something with such impact and sustainability? A building leader has the aptitude to see the landscape differently, to know what can be rather than what is. They often spend significant time in thinking mode, delve into research, tap into resources, and ask endless questions. A leader of this nature has the gift to convince others of the opportunity and is not surprised, nor hindered, when colliding with adversity. Their strength is putting together the infrastructure and empowering others to carry out the job, while staying tethered to the bigger picture. Neither age nor title defines this leader, as the aspiration to build may be applied to any sized effort, whether a team, a project, or a company. Not everyone fits the mold, but when you sink your teeth into this leadership style, you forever change the scenery.

Fortitude

Beneath the mounds of leafy compost, amongst the rotting logs, and from within the loose soil along the fringe of the walking trail emerge the bark centipedes. These little reddish-brown invertebrates are equipped with a set of venomous legs and lethal stout jaws but, alas, lack a backbone.

As a leader do you possess a backbone? Do you have the courage to have a difficult conversation face-to-face, or do you rationalize the decision to send an electronic communication? Do you stand up for the minority opinion or bow to the voices of the majority? Fortitude is the backbone of leadership. It is the embodiment of integrity, character, and mental prowess that allows you to be courageous when facing adversity. It is the conviction to address conflict, the nerve to challenge with respect, the gentle handling of embarrassment, the strength to acknowledge fault, and the patience to understand disappointment. Fortitude is the resolve to stay strong and hide your unease when the easy way is simple avoidance. Honest reflection and analysis of behavior will spotlight your range of emotional responses and present areas to strengthen or improve. Fortitude is learnable. Unlike the little spineless centipede, you can grow a backbone.

Quieted Time

There is a beautiful silence that envelopes the lake when it is blanketed in a dense fog. Nature becomes instinctively hushed, and I find that I become that way as well.

It is a rare moment in the workplace when the environment is quieted, and you have the time to still your mind. That is unfortunate, as any portion of the workday with no disruption allows each of us to think creatively, be innovative, apply intentional focus toward goals, transition from reactive to proactive, or just get those "to dos" done. Research indicates that quiet time improves morale and provides a sense of calm and accomplishment. Forward-thinking leaders schedule these uninterrupted intervals on the calendar, with the same level of commitment as, say, a weekly meeting or conference call. Electronic devices, including phones and monitors, are turned off to reduce distractions and minimize interruptions. The agenda for the use of this time is dependent upon the leader, but there should be a plan to document, recognize, and communicate the resulting achievements. Anticipate a period of adjustment for each member of the team as they work to learn the art of productive silence. Maybe even consider buying a fog machine.

Micromanagement

The sky was rife with helicopters, propellers spinning, whirling away from the tree canopy. The aerodynamic samaras of the red maple created a tornado-like whirlwind as they spun slowly to the ground.

These paper-thin, winged seeds conjure up the notion of a helicopter leader, one who is overly focused on and overly involved in all aspects of their team. These micromanagers have a need to control every detail, feel everything is urgent, and believe that without their intervention nothing will be executed correctly. Whether a result of insecurity, fear, or a need for perfection, a micromanager's hands-on approach indicates more about them than their team, and it is not positive. Wielding this type of control results in a team that is demoralized, unempowered, and laden with distrust, and that may react with rebellious measures to resolve resentful attitudes. Time to stop hovering.

Recognize your role is to lead to the bigger picture, to focus on outcomes and not processes. Praise more, criticize less, talk less, listen more. Communicate expectations and give your team space; allow new seeds to take flight. Stepping back will be difficult at first, but small changes in direction will help you to land that helicopter.

Frustration

The grassy reeds nestled along the lake's edge swayed in the gentle breeze as the sun's glitter scattered diamonds on the rippling water. The relaxing, peaceful moment was all too soon intruded upon by the jackhammer-like drilling of a pileated woodpecker. It is a wonder of nature that pecking up to 20 times per second causes no impact to the woodpecker's brain, for when a leader beats their head against the wall a headache quickly ensues.

Being frustrated, a common workplace problem, serves as an early warning sign that something is out of balance, and it is critical to determine the source. Unaddressed frustrations lead to cynicism, loss of productivity, the spread of negativity, and ultimately turnover. Creating a culture of trust and open communication is a proactive measure; however, once you observe a team member exhibiting some form of frustration, it is important to put focus on the issue, employ your listening skills, acknowledge their voice, and collectively explore possible solutions sooner than later. Or, you can choose to ignore this advice and simply stand in the corner beating your head against the wall. Do you think you can do it 20 times per second?

Public Speaking

In the summer twilight, stars dropped from the sky and formed new constellations that hovered above the meadow. The twinkle of the big dipper fireflies mesmerized as their natural bioluminescence produced a spectacular light show.

When the center of attention, does your team captivate like these little flying beetles? Some will revel in the opportunity, while others will find it a distasteful chore. Confidence to speak in public requires preparation, practice, and presence. As the topic expert, the speaker has the responsibility to inform and the opportunity to influence, but to do so they must control what the audience hears. Coach your team to write down their three critical points and build the narrative on this foundation. The message will stay on point and be heard. Practice, equally important to preparation, is often ignored. Consider the ratio of time spent to create vs. practice. Repetition of performance will improve timing, pace, and tone, as well as reduce nerves. And on presentation day, intentional presence will positively affect body language and ensure direct eye contact. With the proper investment of time and effort, everyone will have the right energy to show up and the confidence to light up the room.

Vision

The light fades, shadows build, and the forest slowly darkens. Chills run down my spine, either from the coverlet of cold air that encircles me as the sun descends, or the deep, haunting hoots of the great horned owl. In the darkness I am unable to locate the bird in the treetops, but I know that it easily spots me. Owls are incapable of seeing anything clearly within a few inches of their eyes, but their far afield vision is excellent.

Pause and consider your field of vision—do you lead with an eye for what is ahead? A visionary leader has an idea of what can be, communicates in a manner that inspires and motivates, knows how to push the existing boundaries of innovation and resources, and anticipates disruptions—and will ultimately do what is necessary to deliver results. This leader is not autocratic, but rather creates an environment that welcomes contributions from others. Sharing the vision is critical, as it provides a sense of direction and meaning, something invaluable to all contributors. You, like the owl, have the capacity to look forward with binocular vision—do so, and you will wisely bring the future into focus.

Hiding

The first rays of the morning sun break the plane of the eastern ridge, casting a golden light across the tops of the tallest trees. At first glance, there appears to be black splotches amongst these bare treetops, but as light overtakes the dark, the shapes transform into the bodies of a flock of wild turkeys. Roosted in the trees, the birds are hiding from predators.

The scene is oddly reminiscent of leaders who hide in their offices, out of reach from their own teams. All too often leaders shut their doors, a possible indication of insecurity or feeling of superiority. This intentional disconnect builds unnecessary walls, deflates team morale, and reduces trust. Do you take the time for impromptu hallway conversations, have coffee in the breakroom, or connect with frontline employees? These simple actions will make a world of difference in positivity and performance.

For remote workers, commit to "visual" conference calls; provide eye-to-eye contact and a true sense of connection. Visible leaders build respect and reduce turnover, and in times of challenge provide confidence and calm. There is much to gain by keeping the door open. Unlike the turkey's predators, your team is not out to get you.

Listening

Entering the woods, I see deep within the shadowed understory a doe and her two spotted fawns. Heads down, quietly grazing, the three appear oblivious to their surroundings; however, as a twig cracks underfoot, the reverberating sound causes them to flee. The deer use their keen sense of hearing to survive.

In the workplace, listening is a less prominent skill as that found in nature, but if employed it can better your chances of survival. Too often leaders blame the pressures of the job or the intrusion of technology, which cause them to multitask rather than provide undivided attention. In fact, it is the leader to blame. A leader who values listening will gift time to the speaker, listen without interruption, and not redirect the conversation to the topic of themself. Both eyes and ears should be employed in the process: direct eye contact to communicate sincere interest and observation to interpret body language. The commitment to be a sincere listener will develop stronger relationships born from respect and built within an environment of trust. In nature, listening is instinctual. See if you can develop the skill as well, for in that split second…you may hear something.

Gratitude

Heat and humidity had a summer party; grasshoppers fiddled but no one danced. In air too hot for movement, clothes clung to a body veneered in sweat. Unexpectedly, a light breeze chased off the heat and cooled the skin.

My gratitude filled the air, inviting the question: Where does gratitude sit amongst your leadership traits? Gratitude is an internal disposition and the genesis for expression of both appreciation and thanks. It is the emotional response to a specific action, person, or moment. As a sentiment of strength, it builds trust and respect, demonstrates awareness and engagement, and draws others to you. It is intentional and genuine, not a public display nor the impetus for "thank you" platitudes. Gratitude cannot be demanded or forced as in "Be grateful you have a job" or "How ungrateful can you be?" Those expressions position you as superior, serve to condescend, and end in animosity. Leading with gratitude through difficult times is a challenge. But as a powerhouse of positivity it will serve to generate loyalty, drive motivation, and be mimicked by others. As a leader, you breeze in and out of people's lives. Do so with gratitude and you will be better for it.

Scarcity of Resources

Boots crunched loudly on the crusted snow. Bright red cardinals took wing, but the little brown bats deep within the dark hibernaculum were thankfully undisturbed. Scarcity of food in winter forces this flying mammal to hibernate, living off stored fat with a radically reduced metabolic rate, to extend life and avoid starvation.

This fragile balance of resources is all too understood within the workplace. The competition for people, technology, or capital is ever-present. Little hardship rests on recipients of these precious resources, but for leaders left in the cold it is a disruptive challenge. Have you experienced this, left to boost morale, and generate positivity when your team feels overworked and underappreciated while tasked with unadjusted business objectives? In this period, transparent, consistent communication is key, along with increased flexibility and autonomy. Brainstorm to analyze and streamline current structures, redeploy or release un-productive responsibilities, tackle unresolved problems, and deal with disappointments. Proactively collect ROI data, impact statements, and research to prepare for the next round of budget requests. These strategies will stabilize productivity, reduce turnover, and maybe offer unexpected solutions. Lead with purpose through the season of scarcity, and your team will stay alive until resources become abundant once again.

Office Politics

Clouds diffused the moonlight; shadows crept across the woodland floor. The slender, furry long-tailed weasel would have gone unseen if not for the bright green emerald shine of its eyes caught in the flashlight beam. Unsavory habits, a big attitude, and an aggressive nature define this small animal and are characteristics often used to describe the office politico as well.

Politics are naturally present in the workplace, as some use glad-handing and insincere behaviors to improve the trajectory of their career; however, this leadership ability need not be negative. Smart leaders build political competence, nurture interpersonal relationships with power leaders and influencers, observe the office landscape to understand potential risks, and deliver on promises to ensure future support. Authenticity is critical as trust builds and personal influence grows. Strategy plays a part as well; forecast support or resistance to ideas and intelligently negotiate through those obstacles. Then there is the emotional construct to consider. Calmly and rationally respond to conflict and disappointment and avoid that innate desire to participate in gossip. There are potential pitfalls of peril when participating in office politics, but doing so with ethics and integrity will keep you from becoming a little weasel.

Patience

The day was dreary, the air laden with the winter morning dampness. Anticipating the absence of the sun, the woods befittingly dressed in camouflage for the day. As a result, the red tail hawk, with its reddish-brown plumage, was almost indiscernible within the abundance of dried leaves. Watching and waiting, it was a figure of patience.

Lao Tzu's saying "Nature does not hurry, yet everything is accomplished" in juxtaposition to today's world of immediacy is worthy of contemplation. The profusion of communications, the demands of deadlines, and the uncertainty of the future cause leaders to be impatient, placing preventable pressures on both themselves and their teams. Patience, a vanishing virtue, provides a greater sense of restraint in difficult situations and allows for more constructive critical thinking and problem-solving.

It gifts the leader with the wisdom to know when to act and when to pause, and it provides the doggedness needed to withstand the pressures that undermine the objective. Colleagues see it as restrained confidence, and direct reports will interpret it as empathetic. Slow down, take a note from nature: develop patience as a pattern of behavior, and others will watch you like a hawk.

Tuned In

The lavender clouds diffused the morning light, the only sound being the songbird podcast featuring a wood thrush. On the lake, the fishing line lay slack, red and white float bobber motionless on the water, waiting for the lurking blue catfish. Suddenly, line taut, the bobber disappeared beneath the water's surface.

Does this happen to your team: one moment floating along and the next pulled under from the weight of workload, deadlines, or excessive stressors? To be a tuned-in leader, you must observe social and political dynamics at play, listen for verbal cues, and see beyond the obvious to uncover the hidden. Become adept at differentiating challenging moments vs. overwhelming challenges. Learn when to stand afield, and when it is time for intervention. And when a situation does require action because that little bobber never surfaced, you should remove the individual from the pressurized surroundings, ask questions, actively listen, and discern if you need to redistribute workload, run interference, or simply jump in and help. When you offer responsive, thoughtful engagement at pivotal moments, you build respect, trust, and loyalty—powerful attributes to carry around in your leadership tackle box, right next to that little red and white bobber.

Anger

The afternoon air had a languid disposition as nature napped under the midday sun. Near lulled into sleep, I swatted lazily at an insect, and the mistake was made— not a fly, but a hornet. The normally shy insect, detecting a threat, became aggressive, launching a fierce attack.

So goes the workplace scenario: a simple situation becomes a conflict, emotions escalate, and anger flies. Leaders must learn how to respond to anger—not an easy task given the brain is wired to first react to emotions (amygdala) and secondarily to make judgments (cortex). The trick is to take a beat. Formulate a relaxation technique to allow time for consideration of consequences and to discern an appropriate response: do breathing exercises, count to ten, or just walk away. Allow the anger to subside, then acknowledge the emotion with those involved as the trigger situation is discussed. Avoid lashing out on the innocent or internalizing, as each carries repercussion and will not resolve the situation. Watch out for passive-aggressive behavioral tendencies as well; those immature actions can fuel turnover or end careers. And understand, whenever you do get as mad as a hornet, the ability to sting does not mean you should.

Luck

The tall, thin leaves within the yellow daffodil patch served as a quaint restaurant for the loveliness of ladybugs gathered for afternoon luncheon. They were dressed in shades of red, yellow, and orange with distinguishing droplets of black and white. What luck to come upon this sight, as these little armored beetles are a symbol of good luck.

At some point in your career you have known a lucky leader, that individual who seems to have risen faster than others, promoted without equal contribution or because of a nepotistic relationship. Or were they? What you thought was luck may have resulted from taking more chances, working the right relationships, or putting in smarter effort. Research presents numerous actions linked to luck; e.g., humility, generosity, positivity, sacrifice, learning, etc. One pivotal point is attitude: If you believe you have no control over situations, your actions will mirror that thought and you will demonstrate less effort. Less effort will equate to less success, and then you will have bad luck. Do not rely on having more luck than sense. Look for opportunities, do the work, and, just maybe, a ladybug will land on you for a little bit of true luck.

Adaptability

The racoon was almost indiscernible in the vacant light of the new moon. Indifferent to the symphony of city sounds, he boldly scampered down the alley and climbed atop the trash can, knocking it over. Easily removing the lid, he carelessly littered the street while scrounging for dinner. Unlike other animals, raccoons found a way to thrive equally well in both urban and rural environments. Their adaptability concreted their survival, a worthwhile lesson to human leaders.

The world is increasingly complex, and we live in a state of constant change. Adaptive leaders are comfortable in moving beyond their comfort zone. They embrace the philosophy of rule-breaking to discover solutions and advances. They easily change course, disrupt daily routines, experiment with communication styles, and seek out talent to adjust team composition. Not all leaders thrive in the chaos of unpredictability, and that inability to change de-creases relevancy. Investigate the concept of an adaptability quotient, improve cognitive functions, reignite curiosity, and work on stressor reactions. Being an adaptable leader will help you withstand the mean streets of change, and if you, oh, dig through your trash, you may just find a big idea you once tossed aside.

Letting Go

The old beam bridge provides for safe crossing over the rushing stream. It is a tranquil spot deep in the woods, made more idyllic in the silver light of the falling snow. As it is early, and the trail is devoid of others, there is no hurry to leave this place. Transfixed on the moving water, I watch as nature's debris—broken twigs and dead leaves—are carried downstream.

Leaders need to allow the detrimental debris in their lives to float away. Is it hard for you to let go of frustrations, disputes, and resentments? It takes intentional effort, as certain research indicates our brains are naturally hard-wired to recall negative impact far more than positive. Recognize that you alone are carrying around the weight of the past issue, not those who caused the offense. The refuse from the past affects future performance, and your behavioral responses are both observed and learned by younger leaders. To move forward, determine the source of the annoyance, then work on a solution or acknowledge that there is not one. Forgive or forget is the final step. You must learn to let it all go; after all, it is just water under the bridge.

Digging for Solutions

Within the soft edge, between forest and farm, amongst small trees and tall grasses, beneath the tangle of blackberry bushes and under the wild geraniums, is a mound of fresh dirt—the welcome mat to a groundhog's sette. Built for digging, this marmot is short and muscular, with long, curved claws, and it can excavate over 700 pounds of dirt to dig just one den.

How adept is your team at digging? From a simplified yes/no "tame" problem to the complexities of a multi-scenario "wicked" problem, digging for answers requires open-mindedness, logic, persistence, patience, and creativity. Coach by asking "why" to initiate self-discovery of the root cause of the problem and build a foundation of understanding for the next steps. Encourage them to consider resources at hand and explore "what if" strategies to motivate the desire to solve rather than looking to you to resolve. To allow them to experience the consequences of not solving the problem is an alternative but will simply lead to other problems. Empower your team to solve without the confines of historical assumptions and to confidently speak up. Digging for solutions is rewarding, but everyone should expect to get a little dirt under their nails.

Procrastination

The fall wind is feisty, greedily snatching the fragile leaves from the oak and hickory trees towering above the ground. Floating downward, the leaves add another layer atop the millions already on the ground (an empirical generalization as no official count was conducted). The thought of raking the leaves is fleeting, the magnitude and mundaneness of the project making procrastination pleasing.

As a common reaction to an unappealing task, leaders incur procrastination as a stress inducer, demoralizer, and time stealer with possible negative personal or financial consequences. With no positive attributes, procrastination must be tackled. One strategy is to undertake a project in a pattern of 15-minute daily intervals. Literally set a timer, put forth focused effort for 15 minutes, then give yourself permission to stop. By the week's end, you will have obtained progress toward the goal that otherwise would have been ignored. It is a simple solution that works. In your world, there is probably one or two "leafy" projects that you have deprioritized in favor of something less challenging or more enjoyable. Start today, set your timer, and make headway. And if not, come help me rake leaves, or better yet, let's go for a walk instead!

Teamwork

As the light fails, and dusk settles in over the water, I hear the Canadian geese moments before I can see them. When they finally come into view, they are in a perfect V pattern. By flying this formation, the geese are working as a team. They reduce energy expenditure, travel in the right direction, and keep track of one another. An interesting truth is that while the older birds communicate the directional information, the leader of the skein is constantly changing—completely independent of the age of the bird.

Isn't that a grand concept, allowing each member of the team to take the lead position at some point and provide the leader both a break and the opportunity to re-energize? Think of the experience and confidence this builds, not to mention the new insights that may arise. And if someone flies off course, then the experienced leader simply communicates the appropriate direction and gets the team right back on track. If you are looking for a way to revitalize your team, take a gander at the V pattern. You may enjoy the flight.

Good Judgment

A pungent, powerful odor permeates the air. It is dark and cloudy, and the waxing crescent moon provides little illumination to visually locate the source; however, the nose warns of proximity and the need to vacate the area. Clearly, a skunk felt threatened and judged it was necessary to use its only weapon, a toxic spray. Once depleted, a skunk's odiferous defense takes approximately seven to 10 days to regenerate, leaving it vulnerable to predators in the interim.

Good judgment is crucial to the skunk; however, that sense is not naturally present in every person. Sometimes called a "gut feeling" or even common sense, good judgment is a complex combination of qualities including trust, superior listening skills, experiences, analytical reasoning, and the ability to remove personal biases. Pretty potent stuff, and for most, a time-learned skill. A productive exercise would be to apply these attributes against recent decisions and discern where there was positive results or room for improvement. Honest reflection allows for growth, especially when working to remove subjectivity. The next time you find yourself in a decisive moment, intentionally apply the values of good judgment, for like the skunk, you may only have one shot.

Tears

The picturesque day slowly deteriorated as dark gray, low-level nimbostratus clouds began to build. Nature's mood shifted, and rain began to fall. Commonly caricaturized as a teardrop, raindrops begin as a flat oval, but due to gravity and surface tension, become dome-shaped when nearing the ground. Science replaces the lovely visual of a teardrop with that of a hamburger bun.

In the workplace, there is rarely anything lovely about tears. Often expressed as an emotional response to anger, frustration, stress, or disappointment, tears are a challenge. It is essential for a leader to remain neutral, objectively discuss the issues, and separate personal from professional. Understand tears are a scientific reaction to pressure build-up, and do not interpret them as a sign of weakness or unprofessional behavior. When crying occurs, pause, and allow the individual to regain composure or take a break to get emotions in check. Empathy and understanding are critical, but they can be a slippery slope when dealing with a manipulative crier. Prepare for emotional encounters, but do not alter your perspective regarding substandard work if tears begin to fall. Leading a team member through tears is tough, but know into every life a little rain must fall.

Timing

The rhythmic sound of a rooster's crow rides on the winter air and abruptly awakens whomever or whatever was sleeping. It is still dark, and this free-range rooster is indifferent to the common misconception that he can only crow at daybreak. A rooster knows he may crow anytime he wishes, as the instinctual desire to make this loud, intrusive sound could be owed to his internal circadian clock, a territorial pronouncement, or just plain bragging.

To the rooster, timing is relevant, and it should be with you as well. Research proves timing plays a crucial role in all aspects of the workplace: communications, decision making, product launches or disruptions, politics, job changes, and the list continues. There is a wealth of data that advises us on the "best time" relative to just about any situation, and it is worth the read; however, relating your own personal experiences to your team will have a far greater impact. Cite positive or successful examples when your timing achieved optimal results, as well as those resulting in disappointment or embarrassment. Raise their awareness and improve their understanding of timing, so they will choose the right time when there is something to crow about.

Succession Planning

The colony was mobilized, the sovereign moved into place, and the crowd of thousands closed ranks. The air buzzed with the energy of 20,000 wings as the honey bee swarm commenced; the queen and company flew away to their new home. The remaining hive, left to begin again, awaited the emergence of their new queen.

As a leader, have you identified and readied your successor to ensure the continued health of the organization upon your departure? If no, why? Do you allow daily pressures to supersede the commitment, are you concerned you could invite premature replacement, or have you simply not given it thought? Regardless of the justification, you must rethink the responsibility—the absence of a succession plan can have devasting results. Start with talent, and if it is not present, recruit. Define ideal leadership qualities, skills, and traits, but do not hire a reflection. If potential successors are within your ranks, cultivate, communicate, and develop; otherwise, if unconvinced of their potential future, they could walk out and leave you vulnerable. Succession planning is a selfless act as the results of this invaluable investment of time and energy, shared thought, and wisdom, emerge only after you have flown away.

Time Stealers

There was nothing covert about the robbery; it occurred midday. Witnesses described the thief's plumage as shades of blue with distinctive black and white markings and stated the blue jay had boldly swooped in and stole the food right off the table. Known for being incredibly smart, and sometimes lazy, the blue jay has the dubious reputation of being a thief.

Within the workplace, who or what swoops in and steals your team's time? Introspection will determine if you are on the suspect list; unnecessary meetings, poorly planned agendas, or lack of delegation are considerations. If not you, the lineup could include chatty coworkers, disorganization, lack of confidence, or even boredom, and remote workers incur additional distractions like household chores and children. Reasons are symptomatic of the individual. As electronic communications pile up and social media becomes more invasive, your team experiences a significant portion of their day in a state of disruption, and that does not even account for the time it takes to refocus. Time is a limited commodity. Work with team members to eradicate time stealers; create a plan to establish boundaries and realign focus. Try to get time back so everyone will be finished on time.

Fear

The grayish-white animal lay still, half-curled with a blank stare, its pink tongue hanging lax over its razor-sharp teeth. Seeing no visible injury, it appeared the Virginia opossum was playing dead. A misnomer, as this defense mechanism is not an act at all but an uncontrollable response to fear as the opossum's body enters a catatonic state, rendering it completely immobile.

Managing by fear, under the guise of leadership, causes a team to become as immobilized as the opossum. The impetus for fear management is a leader's own low self-esteem, insecurities, and distrust. Understanding the fleeting fragility of personal power, they use fear as a negative motivator, keeping their team compliant and nonconfrontational. Within the boundaries of a team in this state, there lies little respect and a great deal of anxiety and stress. Coaching a leader of this nature is challenging, as they see their team's short-term responsiveness and accountability as positives and do not consider long-term repercussions. Discuss the positive impact to their career, improved team morale, turnover reduction, and authentic respect as upsides of behavior change. For like the opossum, once the team senses the fear is gone, they will truly awaken and become active once again.

Introverts

The moon was full, casting a luminous white carpet of light across the ground. The solitary bobcat moved stealthily through the field, seeking asylum in the shadows. He was alone. Bobcats are independent and self-sufficient, and prefer to be unseen, traits that are not dissimilar to what the introverts on your team possess.

Extravertive leaders can find introverts puzzling; however, that opinion shifts when taking time to understand their value. True introverts are deep thinkers, thoughtful decision-makers, great listeners, and quiet observers. They forge strong one-on-one relationships, and they may not actively participate within larger group meetings but will provide well-thought-out feedback and ideas soon after. Introverts do require times of solitude to think and re-energize but will gift you with productive, creative, quality results in exchange. Do not hesitate to let an introvert lead. They are inclusive, actively promote autonomy to their followers, and are not easily distracted. As a leader are you inclined to favor the tendencies of an extrovert? Do this solely, and you will be making a grave error in judgment. When ready to green-light your next project, look to your introverts, for like the bobcat, they will be ready and waiting in the shadows.

Unrealistic Goals

The morning was besieged by an unrelenting thunderstorm, creating a heavy sense of foreboding, but as afternoon unfolded, the clouds slowly surrendered and gave way to the power of the sun. As sunlight intermingled with the remaining water droplets, a brilliant rainbow was formed. A spectacular gift of nature, a rainbow conjures up thoughts of finding fortune at its end; unfortunately, both the rainbow and the gold are merely illusions.

This visual phenomenon is often reflected in the workplace when leaders create goals that are incredible to consider but quite frankly unobtainable. Do you take this lofty misstep? If so, understand the associated consequences of increased stress, inferior output, low team morale, and early acceptance of failure. Take a different tack and develop short- and long-term goals that factor in the varying degrees of talent on your team.

Create strategies that balance personal growth and development with targeted objectives to create a healthier organization. Interject some tension with stretch goals to challenge contributors while providing opportunities for benchmark wins that will build confidence and motivation. As a leader, aspire to create goals reflective of realistic possibilities, or your team will be chasing rainbows with no chance of finding gold.

Gossip

The cave's interior smelled damp, the only sound water dripping off the thick stone walls. As we spoke, the soft echo of our words intermingled and returned to us from different directions. Within moments the echoes generated echoes, masking their true source.

This natural occurrence was eerily like hearing gossip bouncing throughout the workplace. When leading two or more people you will encounter gossip. An unflattering trait, it can deplete self-esteem, create distrust, and destroy careers. A leader must not only deal with the source of the speculative words, but also maintain awareness of patterns and behaviors that serve as the impetus for the gossip. General coaching to "stay focused" and "not participate" will positively affect some; others require an honest conversation that illuminates the impact of their words and includes a strategy to address behavioral triggers. Leaders must also govern themselves regarding gossip. Today's workforce requires transparency in exchange for compliance; if critical information is withheld then details will be fabricated, and gossip ensues. Whatever the dynamic, gossip within an organization comes at a cost. Left unaddressed, the words will leave a lasting, less than desirable impact...impact...impact.

Career Threats

The discarded snakeskin dangled from the vine-entangled evergreen, the owner not hidden within the dense thicket, but curled up in the middle of the trail. Upon seeing the venomous copperhead, threat level was raised to DEFCON 3, accompanied by the decision to reverse steps.

Within the context of your workplace, is there someone blocking your career advancement? Someone you feel has misjudged you, is put off by your strength of conviction, or simply does not value your input? Or, could you possibly be a threat hidden in the thicket? Have you displayed a superior attitude, ignored the chain of command, or pushed an agenda that could be construed as self-serving? Pause, be introspective, consider if legitimate reasons exist where you serve as the threat to your career, then put forth specific efforts to improve. But for times when you are not the transgressor, you must figure out how to survive the peril. Discern the tipping point, request an open conversation for enlightenment, create tactics to build benefit, be observant of those with rapport, seek guidance, and actively document communications. Earnestly prepare, so if this person strikes, you are not caught unaware, and your career will survive the encounter.

Unique Talents

The garden was a battleground. With dive-bomb-like precision, three ruby-throated hummingbirds zeroed in on the salvia bed. At speeds nearing 60 mph, the hummingbirds bombarded one another until one claimed territorial victory. Using a figure-eight wing movement, these tiny birds fly backwards, forwards, and upside down. The acrobatic talent is unique and illustrates that something weighing even less than a nickel does amazing things.

Likewise, each person has exceptional abilities. Do you invest in your people and discover those strengths? Conventional thinking puts focus on an individual's weaknesses to create growth; however, the adverse may prove more effective, as success is accelerated when capitalizing on what is solid ground. To have exponential impact, isolate core strengths and create opportunities that allow the person to be the specialist. This may initiate a new paradigm, permitting the talent to direct strategy rather than following traditional models; however, when you maximize uniqueness, positive results will follow. Contributors feel empowered with amplified confidence, attitudes, and unparalleled commitment. The time is now to zero in on the one-of-a-kind talents of each team member. If you do that, you will vanquish mediocrity and rule the day.

Insecurity

Sitting in the moonlight by the water's edge, the night air is interrupted with the eerie yips and howls of a pack of coyotes. The noise is unsettling, as it sounds primal and a bit frightening.

The moment brings to mind the many times in the workplace when I might have heard bits and pieces of a conversation, and being on the fringe, these caused me concern or discomfort. When outside of the communication loop, the instinct is to fill in the blanks with suppositions; more times than not those thoughts will be incorrect or of a negative nature, especially if inserting yourself as the topic of conversation. This is a precarious strategy, as future actions and decisions will possibly be a response to a work of fiction rather than fact. The interesting thing about coyotes is that humans often misinterpret the meaning of their sounds, believing they are signs of aggression rather than simple communications. Do not make this mistake in the workplace. Be secure in your abilities and contributions, and if you hear something that makes you uncomfortable, go speak with a trusted colleague, mentor, or leader. At the very least, you will not be bitten by insecurity.

Resilience

Dew settled on the spoked wheel of silk threads, radiating a slight shimmer in the early morning light. The orb-weaver spider's delicate web was ethereal in contrast to the rusted pipes to which it was anchored. Considered the world's most resilient biodegradable thread, a thin strand of spider silk is as tough as Kevlar, stronger than steel, and when woven can withstand hurricane-like winds.

In periods of turbulence, what is your resilience strength level? Unlike other leadership attributes, resilience is developed through "live and learn." You must experience frustration, obstacles, setbacks, and failures to understand your resilience threshold. While in the grip of adversity, a resilient leader confidently embraces the situation as temporary, develops a bounce-back strategy, and mitigates stress. There is no room for negative thoughts, and defeat is not a consideration. If coaching to resilience, start with confidence and work through behavioral responses, analyze reactions to previous challenges, and contemplate other scenarios. This exercise elevates awareness while waiting for the next event to assess improvement. Regardless of your place in this world, resilience is key to surviving the disruption of the unknown, unforeseen, or unexpected. Strengthen this ability and you will successfully weave through life's stickiest situations.

Negativity

The deer trail traversed down the hill. Marked with big and small tracks, it cut through a natural funnel and ended at the water's edge. The restorative mood of this moderate hike soon reversed with the discovery of multiple lone star ticks that had hitched a ride.

There is no positive feeling associated with these arachnids; just like negativity in the workplace, they try to suck the life out of you. Negativity will disrupt an organization, hamper productivity, deplete energy, erode morale, and introduce needless stress. Understanding the source will direct the path to problem-solving. Two possible culprits are loss of confidence or loss of control. With confidence, schedule one-on-one coaching, devise a training plan, look for short-term success solutions, and empower the individual to handle difficult challenges. Coach up or coach out. Loss of control often occurs when a team member who had no hand in a decision is impacted by it. Observe, listen, and be visible to this person. Communicate with transparency and re-establish trust. Find other inclusive opportunities, not trivial but impactful. For the health of the team, and to maintain respect, rid the workplace of destructive negativity—before it creates a larger infection.

Passion

A light breeze rustled the pines, providing a peaceful, tranquil atmosphere; by afternoon's end, the breeze had grown and intensified into a howling wind. Leaves swirled in the turbulence, and a thick, ancient oak cracked loudly and toppled. On that day, the wind was a powerful, disruptive force transforming and altering the landscape.

Your passion in life is like that fierce wind: you cannot see it or hold it, but you can feel its intensity. Passion fuels creativity, invites innovation, ignites enthusiasm, and brings about success and fulfillment. Today is the perfect time to ascertain the level of passion you have for your career, your job, your life. Are you acting as a powerful source of ideation and change, creating energy in your path, or are you enjoying the gentle breeze of contentment—or worse, stagnation? You alone are responsible for your trajectory, your happiness, and if the passion isn't there…well, then it is time to make a change. Look at a new industry or a new vocation or invest in learning that opens new doors. Be bold, be brave, step out into the whirlwind of something new, something different…for when that wind blows, you will be forever changed.

Feedback

The cerulean blue sky was sullied by the arrival of the black vulture gliding in a slow, circular pattern on an updraft of warm air. With a knobby, featherless neck and daunting five-foot wingspan, this raptor conjures up ominous thoughts. However, in truth, the vulture is vital to the health and function of our ecosystem.

Feedback is much like the vulture circling overhead: many dread its arrival, but its presence is necessary and critical to future success. Objective feedback is meant to raise awareness and provide guidance for continued growth or improvement; however, timing, emotions, and subjectivity will play a part in how your words are heard. Turn off disruptive technology, use eyes and ears in the conversation, be direct and nonjudgmental, and include relevant, favorable examples, but do not circle around the truth of opportunity. If the individual trusts you and believes the feedback is in their best interest, there will be change; otherwise, your words will not land. Your team feeds on rewards, positive comments, and recognition, but they grow from your honest, grounded assessments and critiques. Make time for consistent, fair, evaluative conversations, and no one will look up uneasily when you approach.

Perseverance

The worn, mud-caked walking boot crushed the sunny yellow flower. Undeterred, the dandelion held its ground within the narrow crack of the rough pavement, slowly straightening until once again standing tall atop the crown of toothed green leaves. The lowly dandelion has persevered for thousands of years, with roots that run deep into history and the ground.

Perseverance stands on dependability, stability, and consistency. Are these qualities inherent in your leadership? A persevering leader digs in and uses pure grit to traverse the complex pathways and obstacles that challenge their efforts, even when confronted by those telling them to turn back. They know there are times when you do not pivot, nor use speed to reach your goal, but instead take the time to recommit and increase focus. Theirs is the mindset of seeking the solution regardless of the difficulty, and that includes failing. Building perseverance begins with a desire that is built on self-belief, supported with knowledge and facts, and accompanied by determination. Not all leaders have the tenacity to persevere, and those are the ones who simply move on to the next thing. History has proven the dandelion will never be eradicated. The question is, will you?

Belief

The tiny home was built of twigs and grass, with a rustic interior of dried lichen, pale green moss, and some red ribbon for a splash of color. The comfortable, safe nest was now too small for the fledgling robins, signaling that it was time to move on. Sometimes, a parent forcibly teaches their young birds to fly by literally pushing them from the nest, knowing they will eventually learn to flap their wings.

Replicated in the workplace, a leader instinctively knows when someone is ready for a new challenge and, through belief, coaching, and encouragement, pushes them toward new experiences. Do you demonstrate this behavior? The process can be fraught with fear and disappointment, for both you and the recipient; however, it is essential to remain steadfast so they develop new, unfamiliar skills and become what you know them to be capable of. Define the opportunity and expectation, then lay out the support framework and a communication plan that allows for briefings and updates. Hand over ownership of the responsibility and unleash their energy to see what happens. Push them to fall, and they will fly or fail, as it is your enduring belief that fortifies them to try.

Creativity

The camel and the ostrich marched slowly overhead, followed closely by the chubby sow and her three little piglets. The white fluffy cloudscape was robust against the bright blue sky and provided a shifting spectacle to challenge the imagination. Clouds tickle our creativity and allow us to see something beyond water particles in the sky.

Do you actively invite creativity into your world? Creative leadership challenges the norm, rethinks current status, and sees the transformative possibilities of what could be. It extends creative license to everyone, generates unexpected input, and invites fresh perspective to reshape all aspects of the workplace. When brave enough to confront the status quo, your team will develop more nimble perceptual acuity, discover passion, and drive change. The resulting environment fosters innovation, encourages ideation, and is free of reactive criticism, a utopia for creative minds. But once the environment shifts and ideas come floating in, as a creative leader you must lead through the impossible to the possible. Take calculated risks and recognize that failure contributes to the process. Inspiration, imagination, and innovation are hallmarks of a creative culture. Be the creative leader that asks, "What do you see in see in the clouds?"

Bad Hires

The black and white sandwich cookie cows dotted the landscape of hilly green pasture, their coloring in stark contrast to the extravagant plumage of the Indian peacock strutting along the fence row. Its long, iridescent blue neck and crystal-covered green tail feathers, adorned with ocellated spots, were resplendent in the afternoon sun.

The scene is likened to a herd of applicants with one individual standing out proudly against the others. Alas, hire made, you soon realize the mistake. Owing to pressures to fill a position, or a candidate simply interviewing well, you will within the span of your career make bad hires. The trick is to recognize, and own, the error in judgment sooner than later. When encountering unfixable issues like character weakness, a negative attitude, or over-emphasized abilities, it is better to devise an exit strategy rather than to live with the situation. Understand the financial impact, work with HR, and speak with the new hire as parts of the plan. Unburden the workplace with the detractor, and both colleagues and team will respect you for the timely action. Learn from the mistake, and next time, you will not be so razzle-dazzled by the proud peacock.

Humor

The muddy exit ramp took a hard right off the embankment and merged straight into the lake. The slippery sloping slide was ideal for the North American otters as they slid on their bellies, squealing, chirping, and clowning around. Appearing humorous, the otter is actually teaching and strengthening social bonds.

Do you slip humor into your leadership patterns? There are benefits to doing so: less stress, better engagement, and a boost in creativity. Laughing generates positive energy and produces an environment in which your team members want to contribute. Humor is a useful tool when trying to deflect anger, de-escalate tension, and diffuse negativity, as a moment of levity diverts the attention long enough for calmer minds to prevail. Also, recognize that when things go awry, deadlines are missed, or unforeseeable problems emerge, unexpectedly laughing through the situation creates a stronger bond with your team and positions you as empathetic. The right time to dispense humor is a skill best learned through experience and observation; otherwise, you may appear awkward or, worse, complicate the situation. Learn from the otters: incorporate a little humor and laughter into the workplace as you ride the uncontrollable slippery slope of the workday.

Energy

The rainclouds were depleted; the sun's rays easily pushed them aside. Sitting amongst the rain droplets on a glossy magnolia leaf was a dark orange viceroy butterfly, wings opened wide and angled toward the sun. A complex structure, the butterfly's wings regulate its temperature throughout the day, warming the body to at least 86^0 F for flight or fluttering to cool it down.

As a leader, do you emulate this behavior, monitoring energy to balance harmony with drive? As the initial source of energy for the day, you set the tone with your attitude and actions. A team is complex and, given that any member can quickly deplete this resource, you must constantly recalibrate to achieve maximum results. Understand the team composition and coach accordingly for those that exhaust or diminish the energy, discuss the source of the discord, and explore options to reduce or mitigate the issues. To energize the team, brainstorm harmonic ideas like healthier snacks, develop a passion project, or simply volunteer; the options are endless. Your team looks to you for confidence, reassurance, and energy to face the day, and just by entering the room you possess the power to create the butterfly effect.

Communicating Problems

The early morning light stretches down into the bottom of the ravine and illuminates a small dark circle. Suddenly, the form begins to rise, and raucous shrills emanate from its edges. A murder of crows takes flight. Highly intelligent birds, crows will encircle and study a fallen member, communicate the danger, and proceed to investigate for further threats. Research confirms crows to be superior communicators and excellent problem-solvers, attributes that ensure their survival.

When encountering a problem, do you solve first and communicate later? Thinking that covert problem-solving or aftermath forgiveness are more clever routes than transparency can be strategies with pitfalls. Bringing a problem to the forefront, along with thoughtful solutions, ensures that no one is caught unaware and safeguards the team. The privilege, or the burden, to solve the problem may still be yours, but you are not in the shadows doing it alone. Be proactive in attacking a problem, and communicate with openness; otherwise, if found out, you might have to eat crow—and I know from experience, it does not taste all that great.

Navigating a Career

The Milky Way haze shone bright in the dark, moon-less sky. The barred spiral galaxy was breathtaking in its expanse with over 100 billion indiscernible stars and planets. In pre-modern times, before the invasion of light pollution, the stars were essential for navigation, direction, and survival.

In your career, what do you look to for help in orienting your path? For my generation, and certainly my gender, there was a dark hole of resources and mentors. Careers were built on hard work and occasional opportunities, but not necessarily guidance or intention. That is no longer the case. There is now unlimited access to information, as well as a plethora of mentors and coaches to provide thoughtful inquiry to avoid costly career mistakes. To direct your future, create a plan, be purposeful, and invest time in researching organizations and their cultures; match corporate value propositions and interests with those of your own. Identify your top 10 ideal companies, and spend time interacting in their social space and connecting with both their leadership and recruiters. Be resolute in your intention; chart a course and navigate toward greater leadership opportunities. Someday you will look back and appreciate the incredible star trail you created.

Loss

The little white egg of the mourning dove lay unbroken amongst the bits of limestone and shale scattered on the trail. The white pine exhaled the soft, mournful lament of the nesting parent somewhere high within its branches. Sadness washed over me for the loss of this gift of nature.

Within your career, you may experience loss of responsibility, position, or personal power. To lead through the disappointment requires courage, resilience, and humility. Process your initial emotional response before reacting or engaging. Reflect and consider your actions to determine personal culpability attached to the loss. If honest introspection illuminates' opportunities for change, then seek out a mentor or coach and execute a personal brand analysis or a 360 for enlightenment. The loss will have a silver lining and allow you to pivot before more dire consequences occur. For times when the disposition is not fairly attributed to your actions, look at the bigger picture. Does the environment provide continued growth and prosperity opportunities? Are you passionate about the work? If not, you may need to take your value elsewhere. The cycle of life will always include loss, but a grounded perspective on performance-related loss will keep you from being shattered.

Rewards

The soldiers, in a near perfect line, marched slowly across the herringbone path of red garden bricks. Little could deter these common black garden ants as they followed their leader toward sustenance. Having superhuman-like strength, ants can carry around 50 times their body weight and are considered extremely industrious.

Who on your team carries more than their own weight and is a dedicated contributor? Are you attentive to the needs of those individuals, ensuring their engagement, happiness, and resource needs are met? The Pareto Principle, known as the 80/20 rule, suggests that most results come from the minority of inputs. With that rule in mind, which group receives your attention? Like many leaders, you probably focus on the majority, expending your energies on the less contributory team members, hoping to raise engagement and productivity, or worse, assigning less work or ignoring them altogether. Either way, the wrong group is rewarded. With the growing challenge to keep your workforce engaged, involved in, or committed to their work, you cannot afford to overburden or overlook your overachievers. Reward their efforts, or they will march right over to the competition and you will oversee an army of slacker ants.

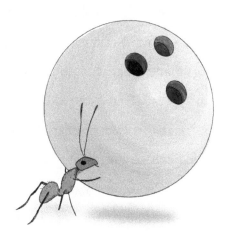

Trust

The inky blackness was overpowered by the emerging saturated hues of yellow and orange, with indiscriminate streaks of pink. For over four billion years the sun has risen. Even when it was obliterated by clouds, you trusted the sun was there.

Whom in the workplace do you trust with such unwavering certainty? As a leader you need a circle of confidants who reside within a haven of mutual trust and allow for expression of frustration, and disappointment, as well as aspirations. Acknowledge your intuition and consider emotions when determining invitation into the circle. Include individuals who exhibit consistency in their words and actions, exercise good judgment, hold integrity as a value, and advocate for others. The selection process is difficult, as trust must be demonstrated to be proven and until it is broken you will not know it was misplaced. When this happens, do not assume you know the disenfranchised circle member as you may eclipse a trustworthy friend. Have transparent, direct conversations to illuminate the truth, deal with disappointment, and grow from the experience. Though challenging, building a circle of trusted colleagues, leaders, or friends will help you face the uncertainties that come with the certainty of tomorrow's sunrise.

Personal Brand

A brown rabbit, a red fox, and a gray mouse were drinking at their favorite watering hole when they met an orange cat. Curious, the cat, studied the three reflections and purred, "I think you are pretty clever; you seem scared; and you prefer to be quiet." In your opinion, which was which?

Everyone you meet forms an impression of you through attributes and actions, values, language, interpersonal skills, or even appearance. The collective of these perceptions defines your brand. If in alignment with your authentic self, you radiate a strong personal brand. But if the opinions are not in congruence with your self-assessment, you are not projecting into the world what you think you are. Pause and envision your brand on a shelf. What descriptors appear on your label that give reason to choose or not choose you? Be brave, conduct a personal brand survey; collectively involve friend and foe to ensure reliable feedback for enlightenment and growth. Create a personal brand statement, concise and illuminating, to clearly communicate your features, benefits, or promises. It takes effort to build and nurture a solid personal brand, but if done with authenticity, others will see what you intend to reflect.

Dare to Step Outside

Everything in nature relies upon innate behaviors for survival. These inherent, genetically hardwired instincts are the same generation after generation. They are what cause a turtle to head for the water, a spider to spin a web, or a honey bee to dance. You too are born with instincts; however, unlike other species in nature, it is through your learned behaviors that you have the capacity to acquire and apply new skills to forever alter your future.

Learned behaviors, such as observations, education, and experiences, are at the heart of Leadership Nuts. The essays are merely metaphors, artfully served up, to raise awareness, challenge perspective, pique curiosity, create action, and ultimately inspire change. But the process begins and ends with you. It is only through your desire, commitment, and practice that you will learn to be a better leader.

To begin, you must dare to step outside. Step outside of your comfort zone, personal biases, conventional thinking, and assumptions. Balance confidence with vulnerability. Engage others, listen, and be fearless.

Take a breath, step outside, and see for yourself—there is so much to learn.

Go ahead. You are not nuts. You can do it.

More Information

For inquiries regarding a bulk purchase of *Leadership Nuts*, or to learn about Leigh's speaking series ANIMATED WISDOM, please visit:

www.leigh-farrow.com

Author Bio

Leigh Farrow's leadership career spanned multi-billion-dollar corporations in the media, advertising, and quick service restaurant (QSR) industries. Whether managing people, projects, teams, or expectations, from both above and below, her dedication to developing individuals and inspiring teams led to impressive creativity, innovation, transformation, and revenue results.

Today, Leigh empowers others through her writing and Animated Wisdom speaker series. She is driven to inform, inspire, and ignite people's passion for their leadership journey, as well as the growth of their personal brand.

Leigh enjoys life in Nashville, TN, with her husband Marc and invests her time in the experience of the great outdoors, photography, and mosaic portraits.

CPSIA information can be obtained
at www.ICGtesting.com
Printed in the USA
LVHW090255241020
669605LV00005B/376